MIND-BOGGLING SCIENCE

WHAT CAME BEFORE THE BIG BANG?

AND 50 MORE SCIENCE QUESTIONS TO BLOW YOUR MIND

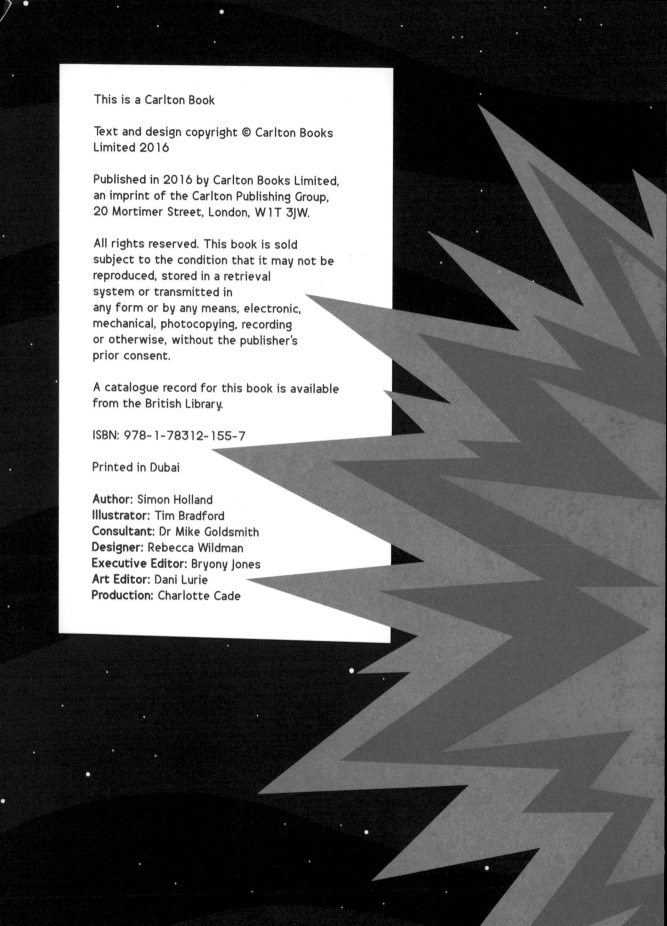

This is a Carlton Book

Text and design copyright © Carlton Books
Limited 2016

Published in 2016 by Carlton Books Limited,
an imprint of the Carlton Publishing Group,
20 Mortimer Street, London, W1T 3JW.

A catalogue record for this book is available
from the British Library.

ISBN: 978-1-78312-155-7

Printed in Dubai

Author: Simon Holland
Illustrator: Tim Bradford
Consultant: Dr Mike Goldsmith
Designer: Rebecca Wildman
Executive Editor: Bryony Jones
Art Editor: Dani Lurie
Production: Charlotte Cade

MIND-BOGGLING
SCIENCE

WHAT CAME BEFORE THE BIG BANG?

AND 50 MORE SCIENCE QUESTIONS TO BLOW YOUR MIND

Written by Simon Holland
Illustrated by Tim Bradford

CONTENTS

How does **science** help me **understand** things?

Science is a word we use to sum up all the ways in which people investigate and explain the workings of the universe. Science often seems like a big, frightening, complicated thing. And sometimes it is. But science is also a very regular, ordinary, day-to-day thing. Scientific happenings are happening all the time, and they happen to be happening to you — right now.

Now and again, you'll be told how things work, or someone will show you the science behind what's going on. But sometimes you'll have to do a bit of investigation for yourself — and this isn't always as scary or difficult as it sounds. In fact, it can be rather exciting.

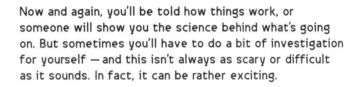

This book asks some of the questions that you may already have asked yourself — questions about plants, animals and the human body, about things that happen at home or in vehicles, about the planet you live on and other places in the universe.

As you read these questions, and think about the answers, you'll come across some new words, scientific rules, theories and concepts (ideas) that will help you to build your knowledge and unlock some of the other bits of science that have been boggling your mind. And here's the main rule of science in this book: have fun while you're doing it.

PART ONE

ME AND MY BODY

Why does my heart race when I'm nervous?

If you run into danger — or you have a thought that makes you worry — your body starts to prepare you for a response to this potential emergency.

You have a peripheral nervous system (PNS), which carries information to and from your brain and spinal cord. This is rather clever. It contains nerves which are autonomic — they can communicate with organs and glands in your body without you being aware of it, keeping your heart beating, for example.

One section of these autonomic nerves is the sympathetic nerves. These look after the changes that your body makes to cope with stress or emergencies. In a worrying situation, your sympathetic nerves automatically co-ordinate some adjustments.

For example, the muscles in your eyes will immediately relax, so that the pupils can widen to take in more light and visual information about what's going on around you.

Also, your sympathetic nerves release something called adrenaline, which makes your heart start to beat more rapidly. This is to pump more blood around the body, so that more oxygen and glucose energy can be delivered to your muscles. Your blood vessels will relax and open up, to make sure the blood gets to where it needs to go.

These adjustments combine to allow your muscles to be used more rapidly, and with greater force, if you need to do something — quickly — to escape from danger. This is why your heart beats faster when you're nervous. It's known as your fight or flight responses.

Meanwhile, the less urgent tasks of the body, such as digesting food, are put on hold, so that the body can concentrate on emergency tasks.

Will eating my bogies make me ill?

Bogies are stodgy bits of nasal mucus. They are made of water and a substance called mucin, which is a protein.

We all swallow a certain amount of the mucus that lines our nose and mouth. The mucus does the important job of trapping particles and pathogens (nasty microbes) as they enter the body in the air we inhale (breathe in). So, by swallowing mucus, we're also consuming some of these tiny, microbial invaders.

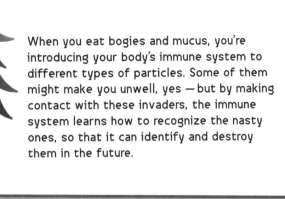

When you eat bogies and mucus, you're introducing your body's immune system to different types of particles. Some of them might make you unwell, yes — but by making contact with these invaders, the immune system learns how to recognize the nasty ones, so that it can identify and destroy them in the future.

BUT... there are some downsides to being a constant nose-picker.

Putting your fingers up your nose coats them with inhaled microbes, which you might then pass on to others when you touch objects. Although your body might be happy dealing with your own particles, you could pass some nasty bacteria, or a virus, on to someone else. And that person might not have developed the right kind of immune responses for fighting the microbes.

Also, repeated nose-delving can damage the cartilage that separates your nostrils, and it increases the risk of nosebleeds. You can cause nasal infections, too, by bringing microbes and fungi into direct contact with the sensitive tissues of the upper nasal passages.

Why is the brain such a peculiar shape?

When brains first developed in animals, they were fairly simple collections of nerve cells that helped animals to move around, sense their environment, find food and survive.

As humans have evolved, they have become much more complicated — with amazing abilities, communication skills and intelligence. To handle all of this information, modern human brains are bigger than those of pre-humans. So why haven't our heads become giant, full of grey matter?

HOMO HABILIS

HOMO ERECTUS

Well, our heads have stayed at a sensible size because of how we are born. Humans have developed from primates. Primates have small pelvises (the part of the skeleton that joins the legs to the spine). When babies are born, their heads have to be small enough to fit through the birth canal within this small pelvis.

But inside our heads, over time, the upper and most complex parts of the brain — where all of our most complicated thinking and processing goes on — have become deeply folded and convoluted.

Convoluted means intricate, complicated, twisted, folded and coiled. This peculiar folded, twisted brain shape increases the surface area of the brain within your head. Clever, eh?

AUSTRALOPITHECUS AFRICANUS

HOMO SAPIENS

HOMO NEANDERTHALENSIS

What are pins and needles?

Whenever you rest in a slightly cramped position and put pressure on a certain part of your body, you cut off the blood supply to the nerves in that area. This means the nerves are unable to send their signals to the spinal cord and brain, and you start to lose feeling in the affected body parts.

If your hands, feet or limbs stay in this position for a while, the pins and needles start to attack. You might feel them as prickling or burning sensations in the toes and feet, or even as shooting pains travelling through a whole arm or leg. What you are feeling is a rush of sensations as the nerves try to reconnect with the blood supply — and with the nervous system as a whole.

Do you want to know the posh, medical word for this? It's paraesthesia.

Luckily, this unpleasant feeling is usually temporary. Once you straighten out or take the weight off those body parts, the blood will start flowing to all the nerves again, and they'll be able to communicate with your brain once more.

As your limbs recover, you might stumble around a bit — in a little bit of pain — while the normal sensations rush back. This can be quite amusing for people watching you, but not so much fun for you!

Just don't panic, it's totally normal. It's just your body's way of saying, 'Err, you shouldn't be sitting like that.'

Does my body come with instructions?

All living things are made up of cells, the basic units of an organism. These tiny building blocks are very small. Your body, for example, is built out of more than 37 TRILLION (that's 37 million million) cells.

Each cell contains specialist structures called organelles that operate as the cell's mission control centre. These tiny systems perform special functions to keep the cell alive and healthy. They also help the cell to perform its own unique function — its biological job — within your body.

Some cells combine to form muscular tissue, for moving body parts. Others are neurons (nerve cells) that help to send communication signals around the body. Some carry oxygen in the blood, and there are many other types.

So how does each cell know what it's supposed to be doing? It contains something called DNA (deoxyribonucleic acid). One of the organelles, right at the core of every cell, is the nucleus. The nucleus contains a chemical bundle made out of DNA. There are long strands of DNA inside the nucleus of every single body cell.

These strands of DNA are squished into bundles called chromosomes. The chromosomes carry specific information about how our bodies are put together and how they run. We call this genetic information, and the different chunks of data are often known as genes.

So your body DOES come with instructions, buried in the DNA that guides the organelles in every cell. In this way, DNA takes control of the many functions and processes that combine to build, run and repair your body.

Why don't we all have the same fingerprints?

A baby's fingerprints are formed before it is born. After it has been growing for about seven weeks inside its mother, a baby has tiny fingers and toes. As these develop, the baby's skin cells organize themselves into layers.

Human skin has two main layers: the upper epidermis (the exposed, waterproof part) and the dermis underneath. Squished in between is another layer — the basal layer.

As these layers form on the the tips of the developing fingers, the cells arrange themselves into patterns called whorls, arches and loops. There are fully-formed prints on the tips of a baby's fingers and toes by the sixteenth week of its development.

Here's how and why this might happen. In the squished basal layer, the cells develop faster than those above and below them —this could build up pressure that causes the skin to fold and buckle into the swirling patterns of fingerprints.

The nerves developing in the skin could also play a part in this, by tugging on the different layers of skin cells as the tiny structures all jostle for position.

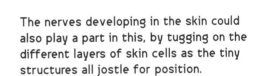

The folding and buckling of cells in developing skin is entirely random. Although we can't be sure, it SEEMS to produce a completely different fingerprint in each person. This is why we say that fingerprints are unique.

Why is my **poo** **brown** and my **wee** **yellow?**

The food and drink we consume comes in a rainbow of colours... so why does it come out of our bodies in such dull, boring shades?

Materials in your body — including the stuff in your food — are constantly getting broken down into other forms. For example, an orangey-yellow substance called bilirubin is formed when your red blood cells get worn out and start to break down. Bilirubin is a pigment, which is a substance that colours things.

The bilirubin is a waste product, so your body needs to get rid of it. Most of it gets excreted (removed) from the body in your faeces (poo). As bacteria act on the bilirubin and faeces matter, to prepare it all for excretion (pooing), the whole load turns to a darker brown.

Meanwhile, some of the bilirubin gets taken out of your blood by your kidneys. The kidneys are the organs that process your blood to get rid of waste products and create urine — for flushing these wastes and toxins out of the body. In the kidneys, the bilirubin is turned into urobilins — the chemicals that give urine its yellowish hue.

So, these chemicals — or pigments — are actually just some of the body's waste products. They end up in your wee and poo, and as they are broken down and converted they have an effect on the colour of what your body flushes out into the toilet.

Why are more people **right**-handed than **left**-handed?

Depending on where you live in the world, between 70 and 95 per cent of the people around you will use their right hand for daily tasks such as writing. So why are only 5 to 30 per cent of people left-handed?

Scientists think that it is something to do with the fact that the brain is split into two halves called hemispheres — one on the right, one on the left. Generally, the left-hand side of the brain tends to take control of logical thinking. It also processes what you hear and controls most of the tasks connected with speaking.

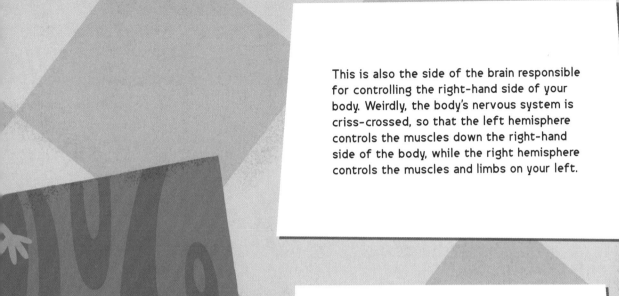

This is also the side of the brain responsible for controlling the right-hand side of your body. Weirdly, the body's nervous system is criss-crossed, so that the left hemisphere controls the muscles down the right-hand side of the body, while the right hemisphere controls the muscles and limbs on your left.

As humans evolved from primates, we started to walk upright on two legs, which freed up our hands. We used our hands and logic skills to make tools, which we then used to make other things. At the same time, our basic language skills also developed. As we gained all these skills, the left-hand side of the brain, which is responsible for them, developed.

It's hard to tell exactly why, but the fact that so many people are right-handed — the side controlled by the left brain hemisphere — may be a side effect of the way our brains are set up, as described above.

Why do I find some things **pleasing** to look at, but **not others?**

'Beauty is in the eye of the beholder.' This saying goes back to the ancient Greek thinkers of the third century BCE. It means that the pleasingness of things is created by the way in which people perceive and interpret them.

But what do the word 'perceive' and 'interpret' mean? Well, humans have the ability to visually perceive objects. Our eyes take in the light reflected by an object, and our brain is the processing device that identifies the object and also gives a meaning to it.

The brain interprets things around us all the time, to work out if they are a threat to us or something that could be useful or pleasurable, for example. This constant process of interpretation and association goes on throughout life. The more experience we gain about things, the more our judgement of them grows and changes.

Every person goes through different experiences, which means we all end up with different personal tastes and interpretations. Life would be pretty boring otherwise!

Over time, you'll develop a liking for some things, and a dislike for other things. Meanwhile, other people will appreciate the same things differently.

Artists and designers study the shapes, colours, lines and forms that seem to please most people — think of the pictures that hang in art galleries. However, many artists deliberately challenge our perceptions by using styles that actively go against what we are meant to like. In doing so, their art can be visually interesting to our brains.

PART TWO

EARTH AND SPACE

Does the Sun make a noise?

The Sun's core is a gigantic, 340,000-kilometre-wide (211,266-mile-wide) nuclear reactor where the temperature reaches 15 MILLION °C (27 million °F) — that's hot enough for the cores of hydrogen atoms to fuse (join together) and transform into helium atoms.

The core throws out explosive energy, which is felt on Earth as heat and light. You would expect an object of this size and power to create a GINORMOUS amount of noise... but we can't hear it.

Sound waves travel by vibrating the particles in solids, liquids and gases. Space is a vacuum (an airless environment) so there are no particles to transmit sounds from the Sun to the Earth.

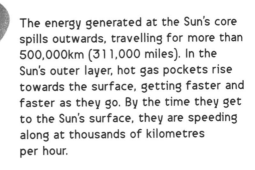

The energy generated at the Sun's core spills outwards, travelling for more than 500,000km (311,000 miles). In the Sun's outer layer, hot gas pockets rise towards the surface, getting faster and faster as they go. By the time they get to the Sun's surface, they are speeding along at thousands of kilometres per hour.

This constant stream of hot, up-rushing gas makes the surface of the star froth and bubble. These bubbles, called granules, are HUGE, spreading out for over a thousand kilometres (600 miles).

Scientists called helioseismologists — that's a mouthful — can calculate what these ripples and waves would sound like if we could hear them. The rush of pressure waves from the core to the surface would sound like the roar of jet engines. Meanwhile, the shockwaves and ripples on the Sun's surface create a vibration effect that might sound like the ringing of a bell. So — 'DING!' — there's your answer.

What came before the Big Bang?

The Big Bang theory says that all matter — everything that exists — at one time existed in a form much, MUCH smaller than a single, subatomic (smaller-than-an-atom) particle.

This miniscule seed of time and space is known as a singularity. If such a thing existed, it would have been an incredibly dense, unimaginably hot piece of material that then RAPIDLY expanded in all directions and formed the early universe.

Astronomers have calculated that this process of cosmic expansion was kicked into gear about 13.75 billion years ago. This has been worked out through observations of how the universe is evolving: we know, for example, that the distance between galaxy clusters has been getting greater and greater as time goes on. If you reversed this process, it would take roughly 13.75 billion years for the galaxies to come together again and merge into one single piece of matter.

So, if we've traced the universe back to this point in space and time, what was going on just before the very first moments of space-time? Some people say that NOTHING could exist, because time did not exist.

Or... maybe the universe has ALWAYS existed, having no beginning. Others say it goes through periods of shrinking and expanding. It is now expanding, so we naturally believe it once had a single point of origin.

The universe might also have sprung up from some left-over background radiation or relic radiation cast out from the Big Bang beginning of ANOTHER, earlier universe. We know that stars get recycled into other objects in space... so perhaps universes get recycled, too!

Can something come from nothing?

All matter is made up of small particles called atoms — and those atoms consist of even tinier bits and pieces known as subatomic particles. Protons and neutrons make up the central nucleus of an atom, while electrons orbit that nucleus. Amazingly, protons and neutrons are themselves made of even smaller particles, called quarks.

During the twentieth century, physicists began to take a great interest in the energy and behaviour of atoms and their subatomic particles. This kind of science is often known as quantum physics. Quantum brainiacs such as Louis de Broglie (1892—1987) and Erwin Schrödinger (1887—1961) discovered that particles (such as electrons) behave like waves, and that those with higher energies vibrate more quickly — a bit like high-pitched musical soundwaves.

This discovery led to another idea, called 'quantum fluctuation'. This says that energetic particles can sometimes suddenly appear out of an empty space, as if from nothing, before suddenly disappearing again — almost as if a magician had conjured them out of a hat!

This phenomenon is impossible to predict using scientific calculations. However, in 1927, a guy called Werner Heisenberg came up with an idea called the 'uncertainty principle', which says that anything that happens too quickly to measure — such as a particle popping in and out of existence — can really happen, no matter how much this may boggle our minds!

What time is it at the North Pole?

Earth spins around on a tilted axis (an imaginary line that runs through the planet from top to bottom, pole to pole). The Earth's 24-hour rotation gives us our days and nights: as it turns, it looks as if the Sun rises, moves across the sky and then sets.

People in different parts of the world experience their days and nights at different times. This is why we have created time zones using invisible lines of longitude. Starting at the Earth's geographical North Pole, these lines run southwards in all directions and meet up again at the South Pole.

This divides the world into 24 zones, a bit like the segments of an orange. There is usually (but not always) a time difference of one hour from one zone to the next. Within each zone, the Sun is roughly in the same place in the sky at the same local time of day — such as 12 noon, when the Sun is usually at its highest point. Because of the way the Earth turns, the countries to the east are technically ahead (in time) of the countries to the west.

But... if you're standing at the geographical North Pole, where all lines of longitude meet up, there is no time zone to speak of. Here, the Sun rises and sets only ONCE every year, so it doesn't appear to move across the sky in the way that it does further south (as the Earth rotates). This leaves you with no natural way to measure the time.

People at the North Pole tend to set their watches to show the time zone of where they are from, or their main food supplier.

Is Earth the only world with life?

Earth is a lucky little planet. It orbits our star, the Sun, in a region of the Solar System that allows it to be warm and wet enough for life to flourish.

This habitable zone — in between Venus and Mars — gives Earth a comfy range of surface temperatures, averaging about 14°C (52°F), that allows liquid water to flow on the surface. Our planet also has a thick atmosphere, which screens us from a lot of the harmful radiation in sunlight, while also stopping the liquid water from being boiled off into space.

Liquid water is important. It provides a suitable environment for living things to come into being. Earth's first organisms were simple and microscopic. They formed in the ocean, about 3,800 million years ago, and went on to evolve into creatures of the land, sea and air. This is why scientists are always looking for evidence of water on other moons and planets.

For example, Callisto and Europa are two large, rocky moons that orbit Jupiter. Scientists think they might have oceans of water below their crusty surfaces. If there's volcanic activity going on beneath the floors of these oceans, and hydrothermal vents, the water could be warm in places, and full of minerals. This would create an environment where chemicals and molecules could organize themselves into simple life forms.

The Kepler space observatory, launched by NASA in 2009, is investigating more distant regions of our Milky Way Galaxy. Its aim is to find exoplanets that orbit stars in the warm, habitable parts of their solar systems. HUNDREDS of exoplanets have been discovered since the 1990s, so Kepler's task is to help identify those that have an Earth-like orbit and the possibility of liquid water on the surface.

If the water is there
— LIFE could be there.

Do galaxies sometimes crash into each other?

Galaxies are massive, swirling collections of stars and star-making materials. They exist in groups called galaxy clusters. In these regions, the galaxies are relatively close together for things so large — a bit like snooker balls sharing a space the size of a snooker table.

Although galaxies contain masses of cosmic stuff, the stars in them are relatively far apart. For example, the nearest star to our star (the Sun) is called Proxima Centauri, which is 40 trillion km (25 trillion miles) away. So, in terms of density, galaxies are a bit like floating clouds of sand, in which each grain of sand is about 50km (31 miles) from the next grain.

All galaxies move and rotate, and sometimes they move and merge together. But when they do so, their stars rarely touch or collide — so a galaxy collision is rarely as dramatic as it sounds.

In fact, these interactions often cause galaxies to evolve into new types of galaxies. This process is driven by the immense gravitational forces exerted between the stars (and groups of stars) as they begin to drift into a closer relationship with one another.

Sometimes, small galaxies are swallowed up by larger ones. Astronomers have observed filaments and loops of material, which are the leftovers of spiral-shaped galaxies that have been absorbed into a larger, visibly swollen galaxy.

Our galaxy (the Milky Way) and its nearest neighbour (the Andromeda Galaxy) are now roughly 2.5 million light years apart, but this distance is closing up at a rate of about 400,000km/h (300,000mi/h). These two galactic buddies may one day merge — in about three to four billion years' time — to form a new galaxy that will be much, MUCH larger.

Is it true that the living outnumber the dead?

This planet seems a bit crowded. There are more than 7 BILLION people living on it. And we're reproducing quickly: the world's population has doubled since 1950. If the number of people alive on Earth had always grown so quickly, then by now the living would certainly outnumber the dead.

But that isn't what has happened. For long periods of human history, the population hardly grew at all. Meanwhile, the number of people who died kept on piling up. We know this because the ancient Romans and Chinese liked to keep count of their populations.

We also have a good idea of how many people lived on Earth before Roman times (before the eighth century BCE) because scientists have calculated the amount of the world's surface that was used for farming or hunting, and how

In 40000BCE, the global population was probably about 500,000. By 1000CE it had grown to about 300 million, and it reached 1 billion in around 1810.

Clever science bods have multiplied these figures by the estimated death rates in different historical periods. They've worked out that more than 60 billion people have died between 40000BCE and today. That's nearly TEN TIMES more people than the number of people alive on Earth right now.

So it's safe to say that the dead outnumber the living — and probably always will. But what about the UNDEAD, all the zombies, vampires and ghouls?

(Don't worry. Thankfully, they don't seem to exist.)

Will the Moon always orbit the Earth?

The Moon orbits (circles around) the Earth because of gravity — the invisible force of attraction between things that are made up of matter (stuff).

Astronomers believe that the Moon was once a part of our planet. They say it was born in the early years of the Solar System, when a young planet smashed into the young Earth. The bits and pieces left over from this collision reformed, through gravity, and were held in orbit around our planet.

That fiery event took place about 4.5 billion years ago, creating a body that settled roughly 22,500km (14,000 miles) from Earth. The Moon now orbits at an average distance of 384,400km (238,855 miles). Its path around our planet changes slightly all the time — by teeny-tiny amounts — and it's getting further away at a rate of about 3.8cm (1.48in) every year. One day, it may drift off altogether.

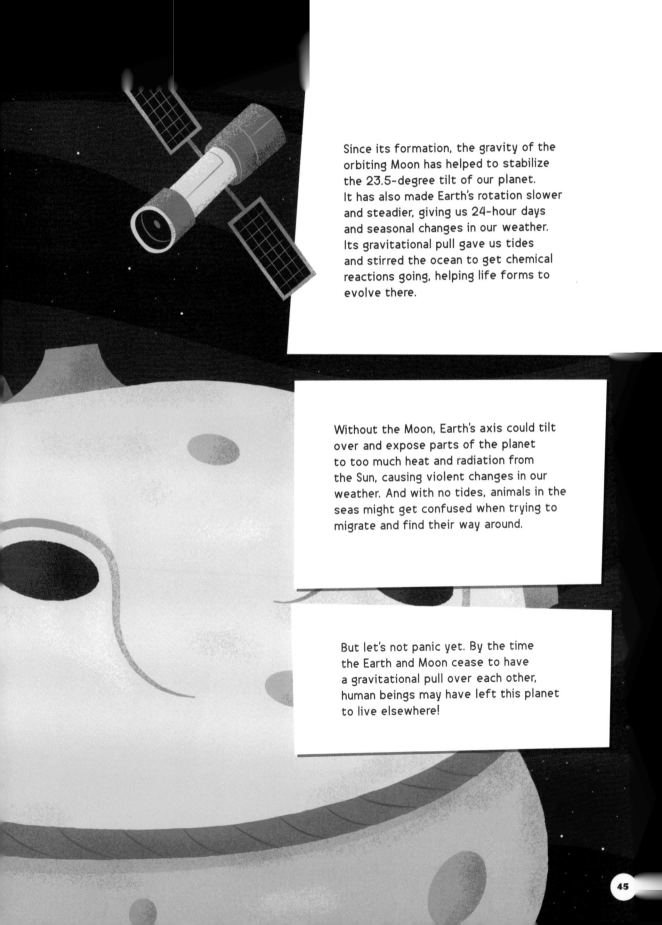

Since its formation, the gravity of the orbiting Moon has helped to stabilize the 23.5-degree tilt of our planet. It has also made Earth's rotation slower and steadier, giving us 24-hour days and seasonal changes in our weather. Its gravitational pull gave us tides and stirred the ocean to get chemical reactions going, helping life forms to evolve there.

Without the Moon, Earth's axis could tilt over and expose parts of the planet to too much heat and radiation from the Sun, causing violent changes in our weather. And with no tides, animals in the seas might get confused when trying to migrate and find their way around.

But let's not panic yet. By the time the Earth and Moon cease to have a gravitational pull over each other, human beings may have left this planet to live elsewhere!

Do we breathe the same air as the dinosaurs did?

Generally speaking, the air we breathe is about 78 per cent nitrogen and 21 per cent oxygen, while the remaining one per cent is a mix of argon, carbon dioxide, water vapour and other atmospheric gases.

The atoms and molecules of these gases make up a huge mass that surrounds our planet called the atmosphere. It is dynamic, which means the gases in it are moving around the globe, all the time.

The troposphere is the part of the atmosphere between the ground and about 10–15km (6–9 miles) above it. It contains about 75 per cent of the overall mass of the atmosphere. It's where we live and where the weather patterns swirl around the planet.

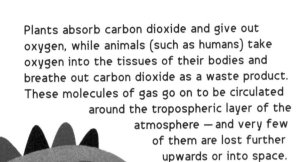

Plants absorb carbon dioxide and give out oxygen, while animals (such as humans) take oxygen into the tissues of their bodies and breathe out carbon dioxide as a waste product. These molecules of gas go on to be circulated around the tropospheric layer of the atmosphere — and very few of them are lost further upwards or into space.

However, over time all of these individual molecules go through different reactions, and get chemically rearranged and recycled as they circulate. So, while we are probably inhaling (breathing in) and exhaling (breathing out) a similar collection of gas particles to the dinosaurs, they may NOT be the exact same particles.

On a chemical level, the gas molecules will have been pulled apart and rearranged many times since then, and they may have been a part of different substances many, many, many times over. The air that dinos breathed actually contained much less oxygen than our air today.

PART THREE

PLANTS AND ANIMALS

Do other animals laugh?

Hee-HEE! Laughter's a funny old thing. Sometimes we laugh as a reaction to something physical — like being tickled. Other kinds of giggling come from our social behaviour. For example, if you tell a joke to somebody, they might react by laughing. But the person would only laugh if they understood WHY a joke or a situation was funny to them. This is what we call our sense of humour.

We're still trying to understand animal intelligence, so it's hard to know if other animals have developed — or use — a sense of humour in the same way.

However, by studying animals that live in groups, we can learn about the ways in which they interact and influence each other's emotional moods.

Apes are primates (like humans), and they make screeching, laughter-like sounds in response to physical contact, such as tickling, playing, chasing and wrestling. Some apes also seem to enjoy this kind of behaviour more — as shown by their sounds and facial expressions — if they are in a more gentle, relaxed mood. Just like us!

Scientists have also revealed that rats are ticklish, and that they make high-pitched chirping sounds when they are playing or wrestling. Dogs, too, make a sort of panting laughter, which has been shown to reduce their stress. The noise also encourages other dogs around them to relax. This is a way of getting the other dogs to play with them.

Laughing among humans is a way of breaking down social barriers, so that people can connect and share experiences. It seems that some animals do something very similar!

What's going on inside an insect's cocoon?

Butterflies and moths go through four very different stages in their lives. They hatch from eggs and grow into young larvae. The larvae develop into caterpillars, which feed on plant material to boost their growth. When fully grown, caterpillars spin a cocoon — or pupa — from which they later emerge as an insect with wings. Crikey!

But how does this transformation — called a complete metamorphosis — actually happen?

The young insect has a gland in its mouth, which can produce a continuous line of silky thread — sometimes as long as 750m (820yd). Using this thread, the caterpillar spins the outside of its cocoon. As the thread is exposed to the air, it hardens to form a tough outer coating, designed to protect the animal as it transforms. Several days later, it completes the inside lining.

The caterpillar then sheds its outer skin to enter into the pupa phase of its life. The smooth, silky pupa (inside the cocoon) hardly moves, because all of the insect's energy is being channelled into the process of metamorphosis.

A large amount of the insect's larva breaks down into an organic soup of proteins, which slowly reorganizes itself into a completely different bodily structure. Totally new features emerge, such as wings and antennae.

Once all the new body parts are in place, the insect is ready to wake up, emerge and become active again. It starts by cutting through the wall of the cocoon, using either its jaws or special cutting spines that it will later get rid of. Adult silk moths produce a substance that softens the walls of the cocoon, making it easier for them to break free.

The insect then lives the rest of its life as an adult butterfly or moth.

Do fish sleep?

It's tricky to know when fish are sleeping, as most don't have eyelids. And those that do — such as sharks and some deep-sea species — don't open and close them like we do. But, if you look closely, you'll see that fish DO switch off sometimes.

In fact, they can usually rest at any time of the day or night, to fit in with their lifestyle and feeding habits. But they don't go to sleep and lose consciousness — not completely.

When fish are resting, they shuffle their bodies along to keep the water running over their gills — the organs that enable them to take oxygen from the water. The tissues in their bodies need oxygen to function, just like ours do. Fish often manage this by twitching their fins slightly, to keep their bodies drifting.

Large fish, such as sharks, keep their bodies gently flexing as they rest, swimming forwards in slow motion to get hold of a good supply of oxygen.

Some smaller fish need to find shelters or deep crevices to rest in, so that they don't get eaten by predators, while other fish have special adaptations that allow them to stay safe while they sleep.

Clown anemonefish have mucus pyjamas — a coating of slime that makes them immune to the stinging tentacles of sea anemones, where they can rest in safety. Meanwhile, parrotfish can blow up mucus sleeping bags, which help to disguise them while they take a break. The mucus probably disguises their natural scent, too, so that predators can't even sniff them out.

Why do birds fly in formation?

When birds migrate (travel) to warmer regions — to have babies or find well-stocked feeding grounds — they travel great distances, flying for very long periods. They need to save energy, and they do so by travelling in V-shaped formations.

Canada geese, for example, are big birds with a wingspan of 1.3—1.8m (4—5ft). This large surface area gives them a lot of resistance against the air, helping them to fly. The wings are also great at catching hold of air currents, which help the birds to fly without having to beat their wings against the air too often.

As a bird flaps its wings, a rotating current or vortex of air rolls off its wingtips. This causes a disturbance of air right behind and to the sides of each bird in the formation. Behind each bird, the air is pushed downwards (downwash).
To the sides of each bird, the air is pushed upwards (upwash).

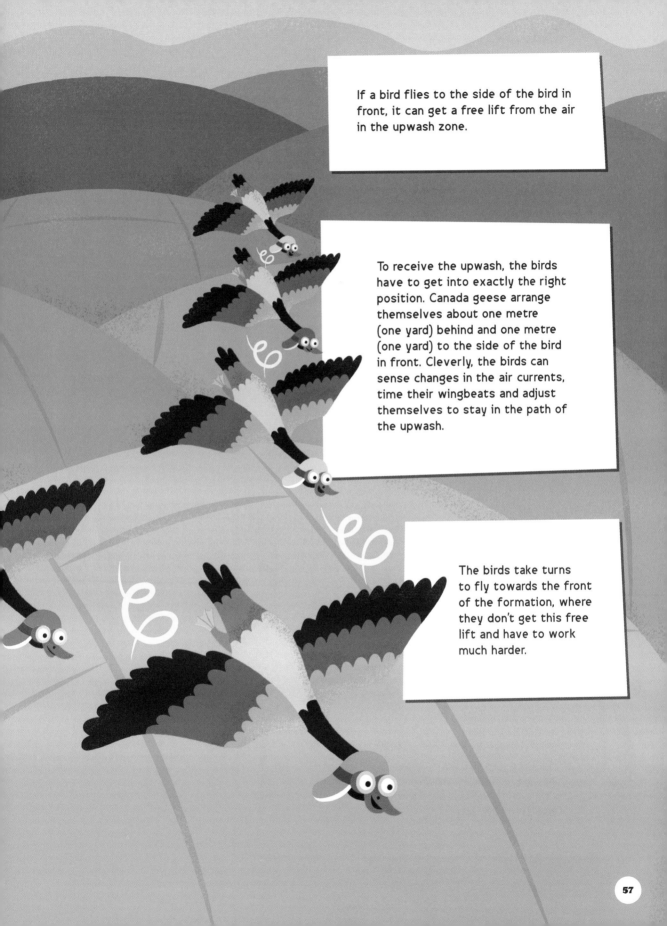

If a bird flies to the side of the bird in front, it can get a free lift from the air in the upwash zone.

To receive the upwash, the birds have to get into exactly the right position. Canada geese arrange themselves about one metre (one yard) behind and one metre (one yard) to the side of the bird in front. Cleverly, the birds can sense changes in the air currents, time their wingbeats and adjust themselves to stay in the path of the upwash.

The birds take turns to fly towards the front of the formation, where they don't get this free lift and have to work much harder.

Can plants eat meat?

Plants usually get most of their water and nutrients from the ground. They can also feed themselves through a process called photosynthesis, where cells in their leaves use energy in sunlight to convert water and carbon dioxide into sugary, energy-rich food.

Some plants grow where the soil might not contain enough nutrients, so they need to top up their energy levels by catching and absorbing the bodies of animals such as insects, spiders, centipedes and millipedes.

Carnivorous (meat-eating) plants have special adaptations for trapping small animals. Many also produce digestive juices to break down their prey and get hold of the nutrients they need.

The plants often have bright colours, a strong smell and sweet-tasting nectar to attract their visitors. Sometimes, the nectar makes the animals sleepy, so that they slip into the deeper parts of the plant, where they either drown or get stuck. The plant can then digest its prey.

Some plants have trigger hairs attached to a trapdoor. If a beastie trips on the hairs, it gets sucked into a pressurized bladder that seals it inside. Other plants also have sticky, hairy leaves that small animals get glued to — and then digested.

And then there are the famous snap trappers, such as the Venus fly-trap. The leaves of these plants have hinged leaves (like a door or a suitcase). When visiting animals touch the sensitive hairs on the leaves, they snap shut on them in just one-tenth of a second.

Do all living things need Sunshine?

Plants use the energy in sunshine to perform photosynthesis, which is how they build up complex, energy-rich chemicals (carbohydrates) from simple ones (water and carbon dioxide). These plants are eaten by animals, and these animals get eaten by other animals. This is how the Sun's energy gets processed and passed on from one organism to another, including humans.

But what happens if there isn't enough sunlight for this to happen? In this case, food energy is generated in other ways, without using sunshine.

In the deep, dark depths of the oceans, about 2,000–3,000m (2,200–3,300yd) below the surface, there are hydrothermal vents. Here, beneath the seabed, volcanic activity is occurring. This heats the water there to between 60ºC and 464ºC (140ºF and 867ºF)! That's much warmer than the water around the vents, which is about 2ºC (36ºF).

The water that gushes out from the vents is a blue-black colour because it contains dissolved minerals. The minerals often build into tall chimneys around the vents, nicknamed black smokers.

The vents are a great place for bacteria. These micro-organisms convert the dissolved minerals into food that other animals can eat and get their energy from. Other animals then feed on those animals, creating a healthy food chain where a variety of creatures can thrive without sunlight.

Why do onions make us cry?

Cooking with onions can be a right pain in the eyes. Chopping them up releases vapours that make you cry... which makes it tricky to see what you're doing. Careful with that knife!

The layers of an onion are made up of lots of cells which contain molecules called amino acid sulfoxides. When you cut into an onion, or crush it, a chain of events occurs that creates a gas. First, chemicals called enzymes are released. These enzymes are now free to mix with the acid molecules in the cells you've sliced open — and in doing so they convert the molecules into sulfenic acids.

The sulfenic acids then chemically reorganize themselves into something called syn-propanethial S-oxide. This is a nasty substance that can escape into the air. When the vapour reaches your face, it meets the water on the surface of your eyes. ARRRGH! This is what causes the painful, burning sensation in your sensitive peepers.

In response to the gas, your lacrimal glands — the bits of your eyes that produce tears — get highly irritated and over-stimulated, producing floods of tears in an attempt to protect your peepers. Their aim is to wash the nasty, gassy substance away.

By the way, it's the sulphur compound in an onion that gives this veg its familiar smell — a pong so strong that it often stays on your skin and clothes for quite a while after cooking and eating, even if you've had a good wash.

Do dogs' **noses** tell us about their **health?**

A lot of dogs have cold noses that feel slightly wet to the touch. This is mainly because some of their tear glands drain into the nose area.

The thin, clear layer of moisture that normally sits on a dog's nose is actually mucus secreted by the nose itself. Chemicals in the air dissolve into this mucus, which helps the dog to smell things in its surroundings.

Dogs also lick their noses to taste the chemicals that have settled and dissolved there. This is another way they sense and sample their environment. Dogs that are actively smelling and exploring will therefore have wetter noses than those that are just chilling out.

So, if a dog's nose warms up and gets a little dry, it could be sending you a message about the dog's health. However, don't panic.

A dry-nosed dog may simply have been lying in a warm place, or where there's not much air circulating. Such places may also cause the dog to be a little dehydrated (lacking in water), which would also cause its nose to lack moisture.

If the nose is dry and flaky, and the skin around it looks red and sore, then the dog may have a touch of sunburn. If the dog has a pale or pink nose to begin with, it will be even more likely to catch the Sun — so it may need to wear a protective pet sunscreen.

If the nose looks very sore or has mucus (or some other substance) around it — or seems quite a bit runnier than usual — then you should get that hound to the vet's. It might indeed be ill!

Which living thing rules the world?

It's humans, right? Well, perhaps not. Humans might feel like they're in charge, but the single most dominant force in the world is actually bacteria. These are tiny, living micro-organisms that exist on the planet in their trillions and trillions. They were also among the very first organisms to evolve on Earth, probably around 3.5 billion years ago.

Bacteria can reproduce (copy) themselves very quickly, which is why they are so plentiful — and so successful as organisms. They are found all over the place: in the soil, water and air in virtually all parts of the planet. They exist up to about 65km (40mi) into the atmosphere, and deep beneath the surface of the ocean.

They also exist inside and on the surface of other organisms. There are probably about 37 trillion (37,000,000,000,000) cells in the human body, and some scientists say that inside the human body there are about 10 bacteria for every one body cell.

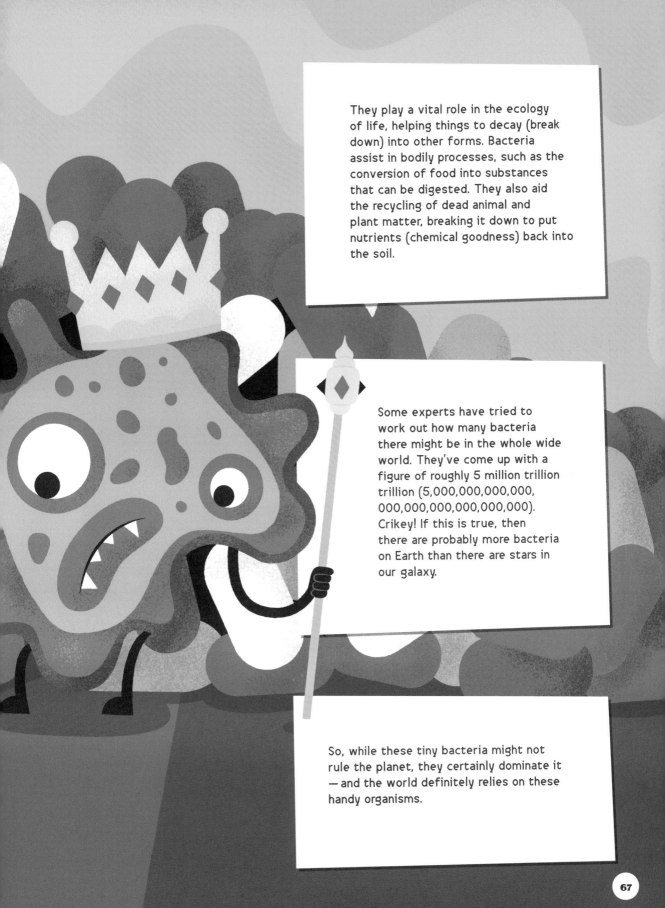

They play a vital role in the ecology of life, helping things to decay (break down) into other forms. Bacteria assist in bodily processes, such as the conversion of food into substances that can be digested. They also aid the recycling of dead animal and plant matter, breaking it down to put nutrients (chemical goodness) back into the soil.

Some experts have tried to work out how many bacteria there might be in the whole wide world. They've come up with a figure of roughly 5 million trillion trillion (5,000,000,000,000, 000,000,000,000,000,000). Crikey! If this is true, then there are probably more bacteria on Earth than there are stars in our galaxy.

So, while these tiny bacteria might not rule the planet, they certainly dominate it — and the world definitely relies on these handy organisms.

PART FOUR

AT HOME

Why is frozen water **bigger** than liquid water?

In everyday life, we usually come across three different states of matter: gases, liquids and solids. Their differences are down to the forces that act between their particles.

Liquids have a definite volume, but no definite shape. The bonds between their particles are fairly loose. Solids have firm and stable shapes. The connections between their particles are normally very tight and rigid. This means they do not flow as gases and liquids do. Gases have no fixed shape OR volume, and can be compressed.

Through the magic of science, a substance can change from one state into another — for example, if it is heated or cooled.

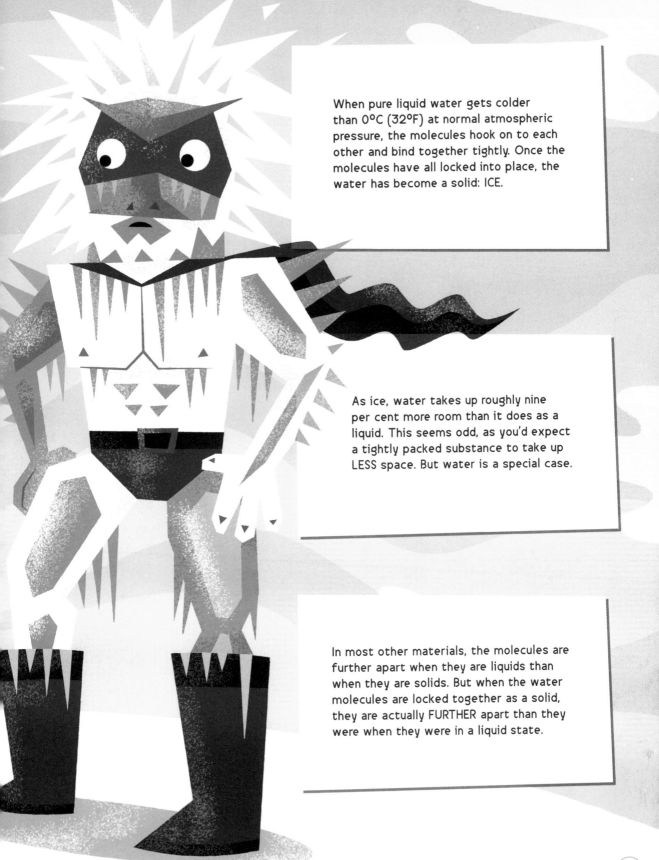

When pure liquid water gets colder than 0°C (32°F) at normal atmospheric pressure, the molecules hook on to each other and bind together tightly. Once the molecules have all locked into place, the water has become a solid: ICE.

As ice, water takes up roughly nine per cent more room than it does as a liquid. This seems odd, as you'd expect a tightly packed substance to take up LESS space. But water is a special case.

In most other materials, the molecules are further apart when they are liquids than when they are solids. But when the water molecules are locked together as a solid, they are actually FURTHER apart than they were when they were in a liquid state.

How do stripes get into toothpaste?

Striped toothpastes come in different types — so the process of making them is often slightly different. Some pastes have shiny or glittery bits of gel in them, and some are packaged in different kinds of dispensers, but here's how the stripes can be added...

The different coloured pastes (or gels) are made in different tanks, which feed into a funnelling machine. The funnelling machine uses pressure to force the different pastes through a round nozzle, which is divided into equal sections (like the slices of a pie). This nozzle keeps the colours separate and guides them into toothpaste tubes in equal amounts — and at the same rate of flow.

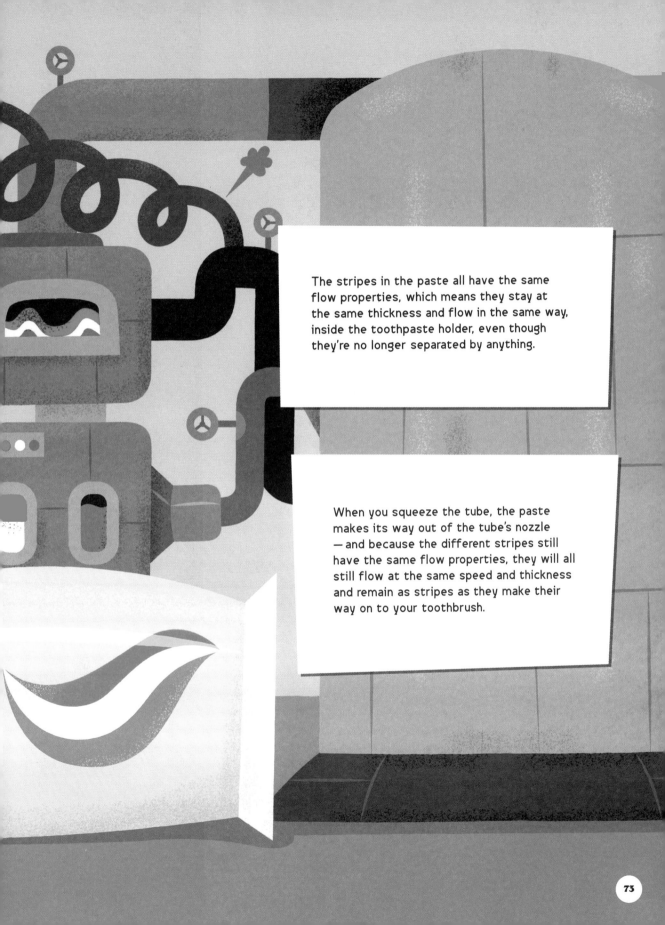

The stripes in the paste all have the same flow properties, which means they stay at the same thickness and flow in the same way, inside the toothpaste holder, even though they're no longer separated by anything.

When you squeeze the tube, the paste makes its way out of the tube's nozzle — and because the different stripes still have the same flow properties, they will all still flow at the same speed and thickness and remain as stripes as they make their way on to your toothbrush.

Why do dustbins seem to smell the same?

Microbes are living things that help other living things to decay. Bacteria and fungi are microbes that feed on organic matter, such as food waste, so they just LOVE to reproduce and set up communities inside your bins.

In fact, it's mainly these microbes that produce the bin odours you smell — NOT the different foods themselves. Fungi and moulds growing on one bit of rubbish, such as bread, will smell pretty similar to those growing on something else, such as damp newspaper and magazines. That's why your bin seems to smell the same from week to week.

But that's just how bins smell to humans, because our sense of smell is limited. We have around 5 million olfactory (scent) receptor cells in our nasal passages. These cells are sensitive to chemicals and microbes in the air, which is how we build up sensory information about smelly stuff.

This sounds like a huge number of receptors — but dogs have, on average, about 200 million scent receptors. Some breeds, such as bloodhounds, may have even more.

A cat's sense of smell is between nine and 16 times better than ours. In the roof of their mouth they also have a Jacobson's organ, which connects up with the mouth and nose cavities. This provides a secondary sense of smell, which the cat exposes to the air by gaping its mouth wide open. You'll see cats doing this from time to time, when checking out an area.

It's no wonder that to these animals, bins do have a range of smells — and they can work out which ones contain tasty food waste, and which do not. Each bin DOES have a different smell, we humans just can't detect it.

What do plants have to do with inventions?

Things in nature often inspire designers and engineers, who go on to create the things we use in the modern world.

The story of George de Mestral (1907-90) is a great example. George was an electrical engineer from Switzerland, who did a lot of his creative thinking while hiking through the countryside with his dog.

One day, he returned from a long walk to find that his dog's fur — as well as his own clothing — was covered in spiky bits of plant-like stuff. These turned out to be the spiny, hook-like burrs (seed-producing cases) from burdock plants. The hooks had attached themselves to the loops of the fibres in his clothes and in his dog's coat.

The burrs contain seeds for growing new plants. Nature has designed the seed cases so that they hook on to animals as they brush past the burdock plants. This is an efficient and energy-saving way for plants to distribute (spread out) their seeds, so that they can grow in new places.

George studied the burrs under a microscope. He realized that their clinging structure could be copied to make fabrics that could stick together in the same way. This is how he invented Velcro® — strips of synthetic (human-made) material that use tiny hooks and loops to join up into a tight fastening.

He received official recognition for this invention in 1955. Today, millions of metres of Velcro® sheets are manufactured every year. They are used to fasten and tighten many different fabrics — from the shoes on your feet to the flappy doors of an outdoor tent.

Why do I twist and turn when I'm asleep?

There are two different types of sleep: NREM (non-rapid eye movement) and REM (rapid eye movement) sleep. During REM sleep, your eyeballs twitch about and you have dreams. The brain switches to REM sleep every 90 minutes approximately, and these periods last — on average — for about 15 or 20 minutes.

It's in these shorter, REM periods that your brain is more active: the electrical activity in a REM-sleeping brain is very similar to that of a brain that is conscious (awake). In its REM state, the brain's motor cortex starts to send out loads of movement signals to the spinal cord, almost as if it's ordering the body to act out what's going on in your dreams.

You'd think that this is when you toss and turn, but during REM sleep, the spinal cord's neurons (nerve cells) are all programmed NOT to respond to or pass on these movement commands. So, instead, your body remains completely immobile.

In between your periods of REM sleep, you have phases of NREM sleep. It's during NREM sleep that you partly awaken for a few moments every now and again. It might be that we evolved these near-awakenings so that we could sense nearby predators.

Your body's response to this is to adjust itself to the most comfortable position, so you don't get stiff joints, and get back into a deeper phase of sleep as quickly as possible. This is why you toss and turn, but these periods of wakefulness are so short you don't remember them in the morning.

How did we first stop food from going off?

In the nineteenth century, we discovered that tiny micro-organisms act on food and drink to break them down. This causes them to decompose (go rotten). But humans have known for a long, LONG time that foods go off, or spoil, after a certain time. This spoiling can change the taste and quality of the food, warning us that it might not be good to eat.

As long ago as 12000BCE, in parts of the Middle East, people preserved foods by drying them out in the sun. This seemed to work for fresh fruits, vegetables and herbs. It slowed down their decomposition, allowing people to store them for longer before eating them.

People have also been fermenting foods for thousands of years — perhaps beginning in 10000BCE. It works like this: certain micro-organisms (such as moulds, yeast or bacteria) are either present in foods, or added to them.

They are then activated to produce chemicals called enzymes. The enzymes control chemical reactions that change the foods and break them down into simpler substances. This process, called fermentation, makes some foods and drinks last longer — and it can also add a strong, yummy taste! Sometimes, the process also produces minerals that are good for our bodies.

The Inuit people of North America live in a cold climate. For more than 8,000 years, they have lived on a raw-meat diet — but they would also freeze and dry the meat or fish they needed to store for future meals. Freezing is a very effective preservation method, as it slows microbes to a crawl, preventing them from acting on the food.

Why does frozen milk go yellow?

Milk is a natural mix of water, proteins, fats, vitamins and minerals. It starts to go off, or spoil, when microbes get to it, turning it sour. You can slow this process down by keeping milk in the fridge. And by FREEZING milk, you can reduce the activity of microbes even more, making it last much longer.

You'll notice that the liquid changes colour as it freezes.

The different substances in milk are evenly spread out, or suspended, in water. This sort of liquid is known as an emulsion. In cow's milk, about 3.5 per cent of the emulsion is fat, which is spread out through the water as tiny globules.

All the fatty cells are surrounded by tiny proteins. Some parts of the protein molecules are attracted to the fat cells, while other parts are attracted to the water molecules. In this way, the proteins act as links between the fatty cells and the water molecules, keeping the fat globules nicely spread out and suspended in the otherwise watery milk.

When you reduce the milk's temperature towards the freezing-point of water (0°C or 32°F), the fats and the proteins start to get closer together. The watery parts of the milk form crystals of ice, and push the fats and the proteins away from them. The water ice usually goes to the middle of the container, while the fatty, protein-rich parts spread out around the outside of this icy centre.

So what you see is all the yellowy fat in one place, as a coating around the watery ice-milk.

Why are some things magnetic and others not?

Here's a brief lowdown on magnets: they produce a magnetic field — an area in which there is a magnetic force. This magnetic effect spreads out from the poles of a magnet, known as north and south. Different poles (north and south) attract each other, but like poles (north and north or south and south) REPEL each other.

So why do some materials respond to magnets — we call them ferromagnetic materials — but not others? Well, we have to look inside the atoms of each material. Every electron in an atom is like a tiny magnet, so it has a north pole and a south pole. In some materials, these tiny electron-magnets are lined up, so all their north poles point in the same direction. This means the whole atom is like a magnet.

In a ferromagnetic material, groups of close-together atoms all have their poles pointing the same way. These groups are called magnetic domains, and each magnetic domain is like a tiny magnet.

Any lump of ferromagnetic material contains lots of these domains. However, the domains do NOT all point in the same direction. So, it's as if the ferromagnetic material is made of tiny magnets which all point in different directions. These cancel each other out, so the lump of material is not a magnet.

But, if a magnet is brought close to the ferromagnetic material, all the domains in it are dragged into the same orientation by the magnetic field. So the lump of material has an overall magnetic field — it becomes a magnet. Because magnets attract each other, the lump of material is attracted towards the magnet.

PART FIVE

ON THE MOVE

Why do parachutes have holes in them?

Thanks to gravity, objects fall towards the centre of the Earth. It doesn't matter how heavy something is, gravity acts on all things equally, pulling them down to the ground with the same force.

That said, there's an opposing force, called air resistance (or drag), which DOES act on objects differently. A feather falls more slowly than a stone, for example, because the matter making up the feather is spread out — so it catches the particles in the air, which resist its fall more greatly.

Gravity makes an object go faster and faster as it falls. But the faster an object falls, the more it experiences drag. Drag resists gravity until the falling object reaches a certain speed, which then remains the same until the object hits the ground. This speed is the object's terminal velocity.

A parachute has a broad surface area of material, which generates a large amount of air resistance. Its job is to reduce your terminal velocity as you fall — normally by about 90 per cent. So, when you approach the ground, you should be travelling at about 20km/h (12mi/h) — which is slow enough for a safe landing.

It seems odd that there are holes in the parachute, seeing as its job is to resist the air! However, these holes and slits are a deliberate part of its design. They allow air particles to slip through the 'chute, so that you don't swing from side to side or get blown off course by strong currents of air.

Why do our ears go POP when we're high up?

The atmosphere around you is full of gas particles — and they are pushing on you ALL the time.

If you go underground, into a tunnel or elevator, this atmospheric pressure will become greater, because the density (compactness) of gases down there is also greater. If you climb a mountain or go up high in your elevator, the density of gases around you will be reduced. The air up there is thinner, so there will be less pressure acting on your body.

You only really notice these pressure changes in very sensitive parts of your body that are exposed to the air, such as your eyes and ears. In your middle ear, there's a thin, cone-shaped membrane (layer) — your eardrum — that vibrates to pass sound waves into the inner ear.

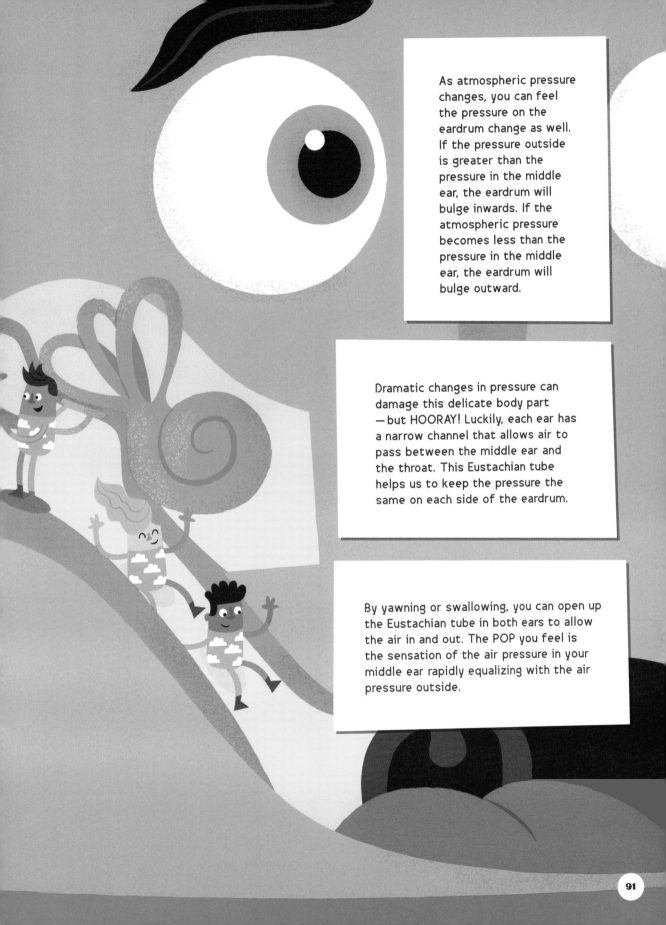

As atmospheric pressure changes, you can feel the pressure on the eardrum change as well. If the pressure outside is greater than the pressure in the middle ear, the eardrum will bulge inwards. If the atmospheric pressure becomes less than the pressure in the middle ear, the eardrum will bulge outward.

Dramatic changes in pressure can damage this delicate body part —but HOORAY! Luckily, each ear has a narrow channel that allows air to pass between the middle ear and the throat. This Eustachian tube helps us to keep the pressure the same on each side of the eardrum.

By yawning or swallowing, you can open up the Eustachian tube in both ears to allow the air in and out. The POP you feel is the sensation of the air pressure in your middle ear rapidly equalizing with the air pressure outside.

Can planes fly Upside down?

Most passenger aircraft have large, fixed wings. The wings have a flat underside and a curved top, which gets thinner towards the rear end. The front of the wings, where they push through the air, is rounded and higher than the back.

The wings are designed to create aerodynamic lift. As the planes are propelled forward, by powerful engines, the air moves around the wings in different ways. The air particles move more quickly over the top of the wings and more slowly beneath, which causes a higher pressure below the wing than above it, generating an upward force. Also, air is forced downward as it moves past the wings, because they are tilted, and this exerts an upward force on the wings. These two effects LIFT the aircraft.

If you turned one of these fixed-wing aircraft upside down, the wings would not be able to create enough lift to carry the weight of the plane through the air. Also, due to gravity, the fluids and gases in the engines might flow wrongly, causing the engines to stop.

Acrobatic planes can fly upside down much more easily than regular planes. When they turn upside down, the front of each wing is lower than the back, pushing air upward —but pilots can alter this. If they point the nose of the plane away from Earth enough, this tilt is reversed. This makes sure the plane is forced upward.

These planes also have special valves and tanks that can inject their fuel into the engines. This means the engines can continue to get the right combination of air and fuel as the planes pitch and roll in lots of different directions. Woo! So planes, if they are designed correctly, CAN fly upside down.

Why do spacecraft get hot when they come back to Earth?

Our planet has a blanket of gases around it. The outer parts of the atmosphere are thin, but the atmosphere gets increasingly thick the closer it is to the Earth's surface. When objects enter this atmosphere, they interact with its gas particles.

A returning spacecraft is always drawn to Earth by gravity. As it gets closer, the increasing air resistance on the spacecraft and the particles in the atmosphere create friction. Friction is a force that generates heat. A simple example of this is when you rub your hands together to make them warmer.

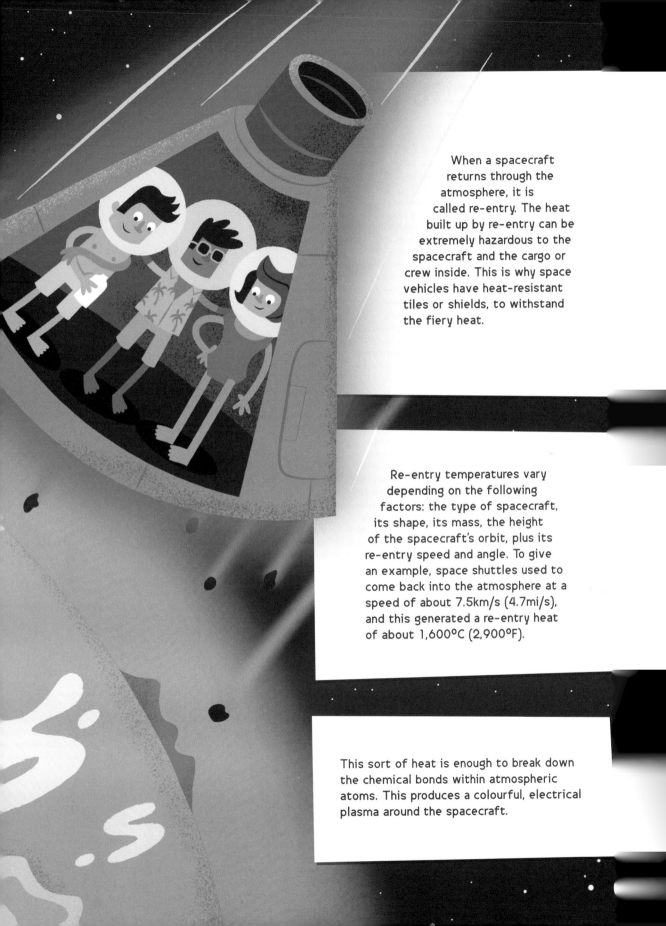

When a spacecraft returns through the atmosphere, it is called re-entry. The heat built up by re-entry can be extremely hazardous to the spacecraft and the cargo or crew inside. This is why space vehicles have heat-resistant tiles or shields, to withstand the fiery heat.

Re-entry temperatures vary depending on the following factors: the type of spacecraft, its shape, its mass, the height of the spacecraft's orbit, plus its re-entry speed and angle. To give an example, space shuttles used to come back into the atmosphere at a speed of about 7.5km/s (4.7mi/s), and this generated a re-entry heat of about 1,600°C (2,900°F).

This sort of heat is enough to break down the chemical bonds within atmospheric atoms. This produces a colourful, electrical plasma around the spacecraft.

Why is it harder to balance on a bike when it's going slowly?

When you ride a bike, you balance on two wheels and use the pedals to push the bike forward. If the bike's not moving, it's hard to keep your body weight balanced. If you lean right or left, you fall over, because your centre of gravity is no longer above the bike's two wheels.

But when you start pedalling, and the bike moves, things change. Leaning to one side on a moving bicycle makes you steer in that direction, instead of falling over. To stay upright as you are cycling, you make tiny adjustments to keep your weight in line with the forward motion of the wheels.

For example, if you start falling to the right, you can STEER the front wheel to the right. This brings the wheels back into line. This is much easier to do when you are moving quickly, because you only need to make slight tilts and turns to regain balance.

The forward-spinning motion of the wheels means that your lean turns into a steer, keeping your centre of gravity above the bike's wheels. The faster the wheels are moving, the more stable you are, because the quicker you can steer into a lean.

There's another thing at play here, too, called a gyroscopic effect. This occurs when something is spinning — in this case a wheel — and means that it takes a greater force to move (or in this case overbalance) something that is spinning quickly. Faster-moving bike wheels are more stable because it takes more force to overbalance them.

How does a plane's toilet work?

In a normal toilet, a cistern, fixed somewhere above a toilet bowl, holds lots of water. Turning the flush handle releases the cistern water into the bowl, where you've done your business.

As the water rushes in, the bowl's water and its contents get sucked away by a siphon pipe that sits just behind the bowl. A siphon is a bent pipe that pumps water from one end to the other, using a difference in pressure between each end. When gravity forces a large volume (amount) of water quickly from the cistern down into the bowl, all the water that was in the bowl is forced into the siphon and out of the toilet.

Because planes move around a lot in the air, their toilets aren't normally flushed using water, which would slosh around too much. The amount of water needed for all the passengers would also take up too much space — and be far too heavy for the aircraft to manage.

Instead, plane loos have a low-pressure pipe (about half the pressure of the atmosphere) between the toilet bowl and the on-board sewage tank. The air pressure in the toilet bowl is much greater than the pressure in the sewer pipe. Air under high pressure always rushes to where the pressure is low. So, when the toilet is flushed, a valve opens that causes the air to rush from the bowl and into the vacuum pipe, which sucks all your poo or wee into it at the same time.

If I run forward while on a spacecraft going at light speed, am I going faster than light?

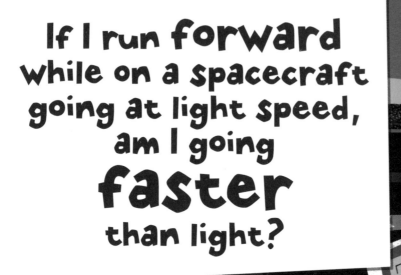

It's virtually certain that light is the fastest thing in the universe. It can zip through an airless vacuum (such as space) at 299,792,458 metres (186,000 miles) per second.

It's not actually possible, but IF you were in a spacecraft that COULD move at the speed of light, it seems obvious that you would be moving faster than light if you suddenly ran from the back to the front of the spacecraft. But it's not quite as simple as that.

Normally, the speed of an object differs depending on who is measuring it, and how that person is moving relative to the object. For example, if the spacecraft was travelling at 20km/h (12mi/h) and you were inside it, holding a ball, the ball would seem inactive to you —but to people watching from outside the craft, both you and the ball would be moving at the same speed in the same direction.

If you ran toward the front of the spaceship at 10km/h (6mi/h), while the ship was moving at 20km/h (12mi/h), then an observer would measure your speed as 30km/h (18mi/h).

But if the ship was travelling at light speed, and you ran forward, a stationary external observer would STILL measure your speed as light speed. The speed of light is unique —it stays the same, no matter the speed or direction of whoever measures it.

Why does the colour red mean Stop?

Humans naturally connect the colour red with certain dangers. Since we belong to a group of mammals called primates, researchers have tried to find out if other primates make the same connection.

Rhesus macaques are a species of monkey. When fed by people wearing different colour T-shirts, the monkeys stayed away from the food delivered by anybody wearing a RED T-shirt. To them, the colour meant 'BEWARE!' — a sign that the food might not be good for them in some way.

Our evolution, as primates, may be behind this. Primates have a strong visual awareness that provides something like 90 per cent of their sensory information. Their brains are well developed, and the parts of the brain that process visual information can analyze colours and shapes to work out what is safe and what is not.

As primates, we are sensitive to these colour signals and have adapted to read them as signs of powerful emotion or danger.

As human society has developed, we have used the same colour to warn people to be careful. Our public paths and highways are a perfect example of this.

In the 1830s and 1840s, rail companies worked together to create a signalling system that would make the railways safer. A red signal was suggested for 'stop'; a white signal meant 'go'; and a green signal meant 'caution' or 'proceed with caution'. Today, red and green are still used all over the world to indicate stop and go.

PART SIX

THE BEST OF THE REST

Why do helium balloons go higher than balloons filled with air?

Team Helium

Density is the measure of how compact a material is. It's how much matter is contained in a certain volume (space).

Materials can have very different densities, even if there is a similar amount of them. Gases are normally less dense than solids and liquids, because the particles in gases spread out to fill a space or a container. Meanwhile, one gas might be more dense than another, due to the mass of its individual particles.

Air is mainly made up of molecules of oxygen and nitrogen, with molecules of other gases mixed in. Helium is made up of very light and simple atoms — and their mass is much smaller than the mass of the air molecules.

Let's fill two identical balloons — one with air and one with helium. Once filled, the balloons will contain the exact same VOLUME of gas, and there should be a very similar number of gas particles in each balloon.

The air balloon will fall to the floor because it's more dense than the air around it. There are more air particles inside the balloon container than outside it, and it prevents them from spreading out any further. So, together, they become a more dense object.

Even though the helium particles are restricted in the same way, their combined density is still less than that of the air outside the balloon — so the balloon floats and rises.

Team Air

Can I swim in jelly?

What makes jelly wobble? It's stuff called gelatin. Gelatin is a processed version of collagen, which is a mix of natural protein fibres that are wrapped around each other.

When you heat up gelatin, along with a certain amount of water, it changes — the protein fibres start to unravel and drift apart. The gelatin melts into a liquid mixture.

If this mixture of water and jelly cools down a bit to a safe enough temperature, you might be able to swim in it for a short while...

The warm, runny mixture of water and jelly is fairly fluid, but if you swam in it you'd feel even more resistance than you feel when you move through water. As it cools further, it becomes thicker, stickier and more viscous as the protein fibres start to move back together and wrap themselves up again.

In doing so, they trap the water molecules in a tight grip. The jelly then sets into its wobbly form — not quite a liquid (like water on its own) and not quite a squashy, squishable solid (like gelatin on its own). It's somewhere in between the two states.

This means the jelly will resist your movement so much that you'll be unable to swim — or even move — any further.

Why do people have different accents?

The first forms of language may have been spoken among homo sapiens (modern humans) somewhere between 30,000 and 100,000 years ago — or perhaps even earlier.

Around 10,000 years ago, humans began to live together in larger communities, to share their skills and trades. By this time, the left-hand side of the brain — the side that manages our language skills — would have been fairly advanced, allowing people to learn what certain sounds meant and then use them in verbal (spoken) communication.

As a language evolves, its accent also evolves — a way of using the mouth, tongue and vocal cords to form the different rhythms and sounds of words. But why do people have DIFFERENT accents when speaking in the SAME language?

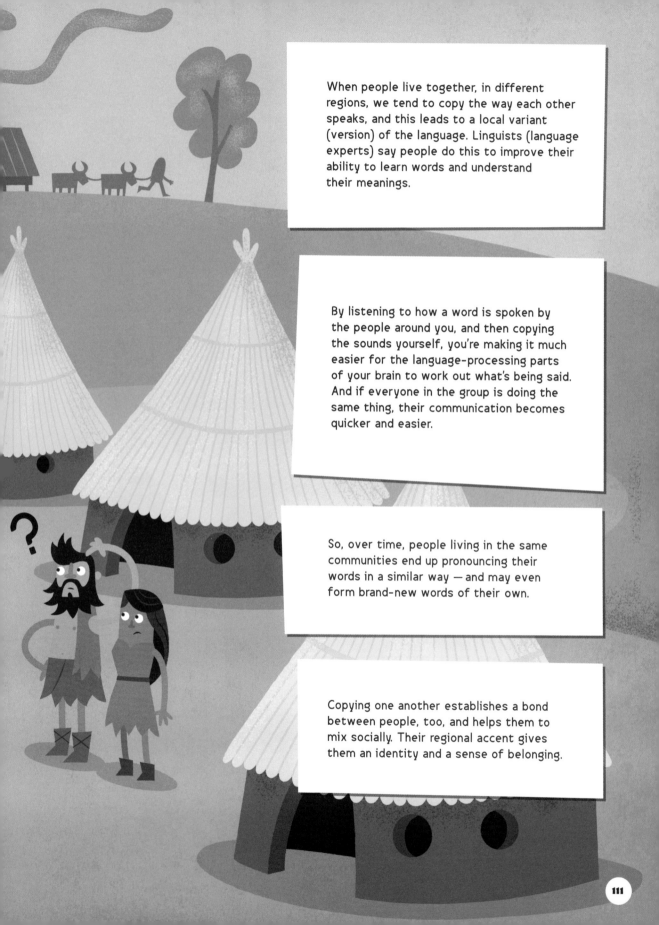

When people live together, in different regions, we tend to copy the way each other speaks, and this leads to a local variant (version) of the language. Linguists (language experts) say people do this to improve their ability to learn words and understand their meanings.

By listening to how a word is spoken by the people around you, and then copying the sounds yourself, you're making it much easier for the language-processing parts of your brain to work out what's being said. And if everyone in the group is doing the same thing, their communication becomes quicker and easier.

So, over time, people living in the same communities end up pronouncing their words in a similar way — and may even form brand-new words of their own.

Copying one another establishes a bond between people, too, and helps them to mix socially. Their regional accent gives them an identity and a sense of belonging.

Could we trap light?

ZIPPPPP!!! Light travels in straight lines at a mind-warping speed of 299,792,458 metres (186,000 miles) per second in a vacuum. It is made up of packets of energy called photons.

Scientists have attempted to restrict light by placing a light source in a container and surrounding it with mirrors or other reflective materials, such as shiny metal foil. Doing this causes the photons to bounce around — from surface to surface — at their usual speed, many, many, many, many times.

But surfaces made of foil reflect only about 70 per cent of the light energy that hits them. And even really super-high-quality mirrors can only reflect up to about 99 per cent of light beams. So, very quickly, this super-fast energy will be absorbed as heat energy by these materials, instead of reflected.

This energy transformation means that the light has managed to escape as another form of energy.

In 2013, a team in Germany created very fine, highly focused beams of light that they could fire into a crystal. They used these to create something called 'electromagnetically induced transparency'. This means using a pair of lasers to cause a crystal to become transparent. The transparency can be switched off again, so it's a bit like opening a door, allowing light in, and shutting the door again.

The scientists managed to keep the photons bouncing around inside the crystal for a record-smashing 60 seconds. (The previous record was 16 seconds.) The photons were forced to remain as light energy, which delayed their ability to escape. But they DID eventually get away!

How do fireworks create different shapes?

Fireworks are made of hollow balls called shells, which contain 'stars'. Stars are mixtures of different chemical elements, such as metals. They explode to create amazing colours and effects. They can be as small as peas or as big as tennis balls.

The stars in each shell are set alight by what are called bursting charges, turning them into showers of sparks. Fuses run through the different sections of a firework, providing a time delay so each bit explodes at the right time.

Pieces of card can be inserted into the shells to split the stars into different arrangements. Once the fireworks have been launched into the air, the bursting charges go off and ignite the stars. When the stars explode, they are thrown outwards — away from all the rigid bits of card — to create the pre-arranged shapes and patterns as burning sparkles in the sky.

Pyrotechnicians (firework engineers) use multi-break shells to split the fireworks into separate parts, which are designed to go off at different times. The shells can also be filled with other shells, or they might have different sections with different fuses.

Once the first section bursts, the next fuse is ignited and sets off the next section, which sets off a fuse for the next section... and so on... until you get lots of different shapes, combinations and patterns exploding into life all over the sky. OOOH... AAAAH!

Will the internet ever run out of space?

The internet is the plumbing of the World Wide Web. It provides the cables, devices, satellites and other bits of hardware that make up a connected network — across the globe — that allows people to access websites and their pages.

We connect with the internet in many ways: through smartphones, on computer tablets, through our televisions, games consoles, and — of course — through laptops and personal computers. Each of these devices has an IP (internet protocol) address, which identifies it as it talks to other bits of hardware across the web.

Some of these bits of hardware can also act as servers. Servers store the information needed to build up the data on websites, and they allow it to be requested on the internet.

All these devices and servers need electrical power to run. So, if there was a major energy shortage — or the planet was hit by a powerful solar flare from space — we would struggle to keep them going.

We also need lots of materials and technology to keep building all the hardware that data is stored on. If something happens to limit the supply of certain materials, we could start to run out of room to store a rapidly growing amount of digital data.

But as long as we have the materials to build the hardware, the knowledge to create the technology, and a reliable flow of energy to power the devices that support and display the world wide web... there's really no reason to worry about running out of space!

Why do boomerangs come back?

A returning boomerang uses a quirk of aerodynamics that will make your head spin. It is made up of two curved wings that meet at a central point. The wing parts are set at a slight tilt and shaped like the wings of an aircraft: they are rounded at the top and flat underneath.

To throw a boomerang properly, you need to hold it almost vertically (with one wing pointing up, but not straight up, into the air) and give it LOADS of spin when you let go of it.

When the boomerang is thrown, the two wings turn about their central point. Air particles move quickly over the curved tops of the wings and slowly underneath. This creates a difference in pressure: there's much greater pressure underneath the boomerang, so it generates aerodynamic lift as it spins, which is what makes aeroplanes fly.

Unlike plane wings, the wings of the boomerang spin around the central point. But the spin you gave it as you threw it, and its forward speed, mean that some parts of it move faster than others — and the aerodynamic lift is not the same all over the boomerang. As it rotates, the wings take it in turns to lead at the top of the spin. And as the top wing is spinning forwards, its speed, and the lift forces on it, are much greater, creating a sideways lift.

This non-uniform lift creates a twisting force, which gradually turns the boomerang as it moves through the air — so that it returns to where it was first thrown.

Can time be stopped?

The whole of space and time has been skipping on for about 13.75 BILLION years now. This is the age of the universe as we know it, as measured by astronomers.

We humans use the movement of our planet to divide up time's seemingly unstoppable passing. We've been doing this ever since we first noticed the Sun (and other bright objects) moving across the sky, giving us daytime (lit by the Sun) and nighttime (lit by more distant stars and the Moon).

Earth orbits (travels around) the Sun — and while it orbits it also rotates (turns around). The Earth's rotation causes the Sun to seem to rise once and set once in each full turn, a period that we've divided into 24 hours. Each hour is divided into 60 minutes, each minute into 60 seconds. Meanwhile, Earth's orbit gives us our years: one journey around the Sun takes a little over 365 days, or one Earth year.

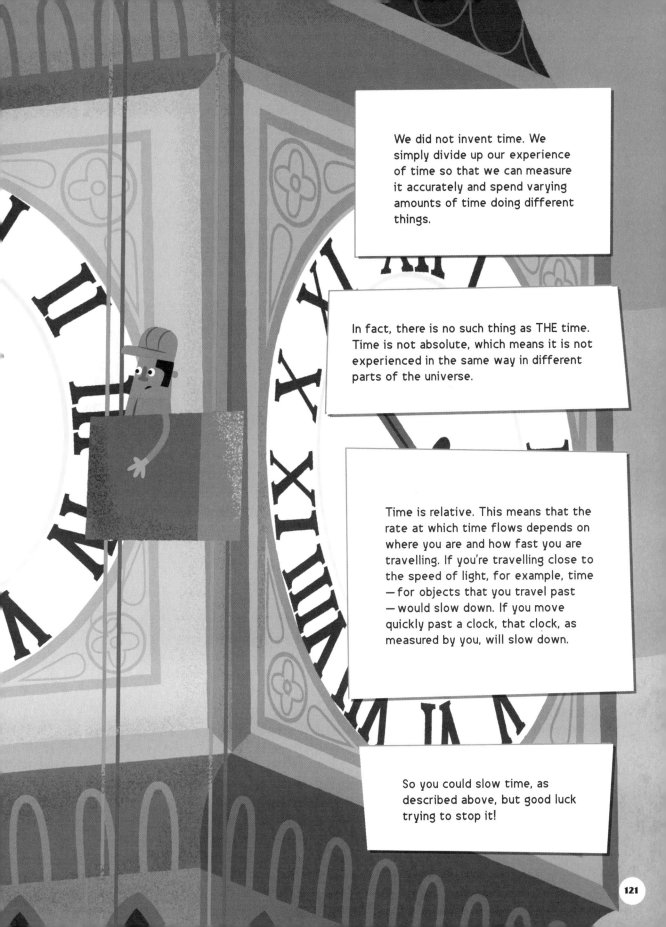

We did not invent time. We simply divide up our experience of time so that we can measure it accurately and spend varying amounts of time doing different things.

In fact, there is no such thing as THE time. Time is not absolute, which means it is not experienced in the same way in different parts of the universe.

Time is relative. This means that the rate at which time flows depends on where you are and how fast you are travelling. If you're travelling close to the speed of light, for example, time — for objects that you travel past — would slow down. If you move quickly past a clock, that clock, as measured by you, will slow down.

So you could slow time, as described above, but good luck trying to stop it!

GLOSSARY

ACID: A substance that has a certain chemical make-up, which means it can react with other substances and corrode (dissolve) some materials.

AERODYNAMIC: An aerodynamic object has a shape that is designed to reduce the amount of drag created by air particles moving past it.

AERODYNAMIC LIFT: Aerodynamic objects, such as the curved wings of aircraft, can change the flow of air around them so that aerodynamic lift is created. This is the force that keeps planes in the air.

ATMOSPHERE: A layer of gases — held in place by gravity — that surrounds a large object in space, such as a moon or a planet.

ATOM: Atoms are tiny particles of matter. They are the basic units of a chemical element and contain even smaller, subatomic particles.

AXIS: An imaginary line around which an object (such as a planet) rotates. Earth's axis is tilted at an angle of about 23.5 degrees, and the planet revolves around this axis once every 24 hours.

BACTERIUM (plural: BACTERIA): Bacteria are tiny, single-celled living things. They belong to an extremely large group of micro-organisms that exist in the ground, water and atmosphere — and also in or on other living things.

BIG BANG: A rapid expansion of space and energy that occurred at the very beginning of time, approximately 13.7 billion years ago.

CELL: Cells are the basic units of organisms. All known living things are made up of one or more cells.

CHEMICAL: A substance or compound. Chemical compounds are made of two or more elements that have been combined through some kind of chemical reaction.

CHROMOSOME: A string-like chemical structure made of DNA, found in the cells of all living things.

DECOMPOSE: To break down or decay.

DENSITY: The amount of matter (stuff) contained within a certain volume.

DNA: Deoxyribonucleic acid — a chemical that contains the genetic code for how a living organism develops and functions.

DRAG: This is a force of resistance that acts on an object and opposes its movement through air or liquid.

ELECTRON: A very tiny, subatomic particle that orbits (travels around) the nucleus of an atom.

ELEMENT: A pure substance that cannot be made any simpler than it is. Elements are made from only one specific type of atom.

ENERGY: Energy is what makes things happen in the Universe. Heat, light, motion and sound are all types of energy, and energy is also locked up inside atoms and chemicals.

ENZYME: A protein that can speed up or control the rate of chemical reactions, such as the chemical reactions that take place in the human body.

EVOLUTION: The process through which groups of living organisms gradually change (evolve) over long periods of time, to become better suited to the places where they live.

EXOPLANET: A planet that orbits a distant star outside our own Solar System.

FORCE: Something that is able to change the motion, arrangement or behaviour of particles and objects. Friction, gravity, magnetism and drag are examples of forces.

FRICTION: A force that opposes (works against) the movement of one surface over another.

GENES: Sections of chromasomes that contain instructions for building a particular type of protein. Genes get passed from one generation of organisms to the next, which is how certain natural characteristics (features) are repeated as living things reproduce.

GRAVITY: The invisible force of attraction between all objects, created by their mass.

IMMUNE SYSTEM: The organs and processes of the human body, which enable us to build up a resistance to certain infections and toxins (poisonous substances).

KINETIC ENERGY: This is the energy that something has if it is moving.

LIGHT SPEED: The speed travelled by light, when passing through a vacuum, is 299,792,458 metres per second (186,000 miles per second).

MAGNET: A material — such as iron — that has a particular arrangement of atoms and subatomic particles, which enables it to attract certain metals and to attract or repel (push away) other magnets.

MASS: The amount of matter that something contains.

MICROBE: A microscopic organism such as a bacterium.

MICROSCOPIC: Something that is very tiny, so tiny that a microscope is needed to see it properly.

MINERAL: A non-living substance formed by natural processes. Some minerals aid the growth and health of plants and animals.

MOLECULE: A group of two or more atoms, held together in a tight arrangement.

MUCUS: A semi-liquid, slimy substance produced by certain membranes and glands in animals.

MUSCLE: Muscles are bundles of tissues in the body, made up of special types of cells. The muscle fibres are able to contract (squeeze and shorten) or relax to move our body parts.

NERVOUS SYSTEM: A network of nerve cells and fibres that carry nerve impulses (signals) around the body, carrying instructions to different organs.

NEURON: A single nerve cell.

NUCLEAR REACTOR: A structure in which controlled nuclear reactions can take place. For example, when the nuclei of atoms join together (through nuclear fusion), huge amounts of energy are released, which can be harnessed and used to generate electricity. Scientists are working to invent such fusion power stations.

NUCLEUS (plural: NUCLEI): The central part or core of an object, cell or atom. An atom's nucleus is made up of subatomic particles called protons and neutrons.

ORBIT: The path of one object, or particle, around another. In the Solar System, orbits are kept going by the force of gravity.

ORGANELLE: A tiny structure, inside the cell of a living organism, which has a specific job to do.

ORGANISM: A living thing, such as a plant or animal.

PARTICLE: A tiny part of something. Atoms and molecules are sometimes referred to as particles.

PHOTON: A small packet of light energy.

PHOTOSYNTHESIS: The process through which plants use the energy in sunlight to convert carbon dioxide and water into food chemicals. This chemical reaction releases oxygen as a by-product.

PHYSICS: A branch of science that investigates physical things such as matter, energy, heat, light, sound, radiation, electricity, magnetism and the structure of atoms.

PREDATOR: An animal that preys on (hunts) other animals and eats them as its food.

PRESSURE: A physical force that is exerted on an object (or substance) by another object or substance over a certain area.

PRIMATE: Primates are a group of mammals that include humans, great apes, gibbons, Old World monkeys and New World monkeys. They share similar characteristics, such as gripping hands, feet, forward-facing eyes and well-developed brains.

PROTEIN: A chemical compound that has a specific biological job to do. In the human body, for example, proteins are needed for cell growth and repair.

RADIATION: A form of energy that can travel through space. Light, radio waves and infrared are all types of radiation.

SOLAR SYSTEM: Our local star — the Sun — and all the orbiting planets, moons and other objects that travel around it.

SUBATOMIC: Something that is smaller than an atom or exists within the structure of an atom.

VACUUM: A space where no matter exists.

VOLUME: The amount of space that an object or substance takes up.

INDEX